WILLIAM MATHIAS
PROCESSIONAL

MUSIC DEPARTMENT

OXFORD
UNIVERSITY PRESS

PROCESSIONAL

WILLIAM MATHIAS

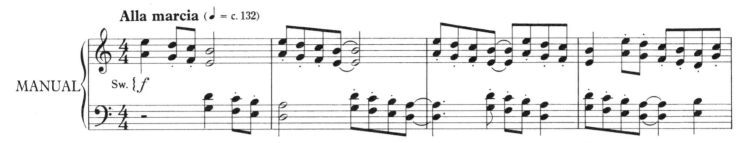

MANUAL

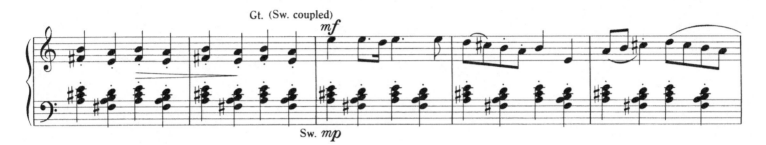

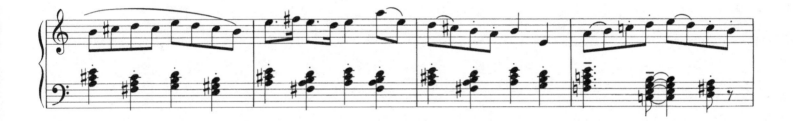

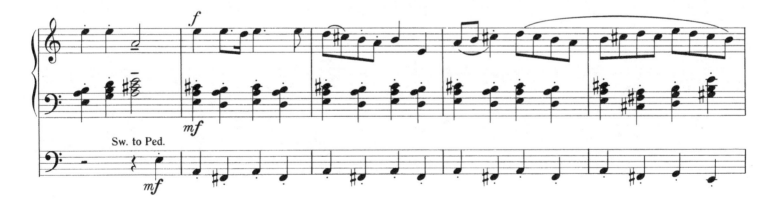

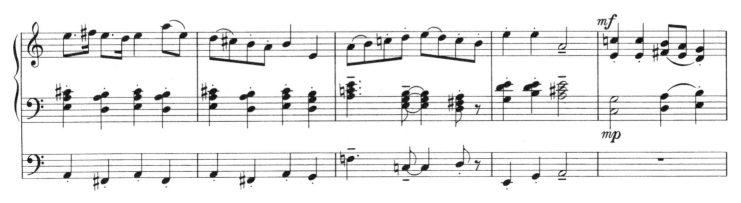

OXFORD UNIVERSITY PRESS, MUSIC DEPARTMENT, GREAT CLARENDON STREET, OXFORD OX2 6DP

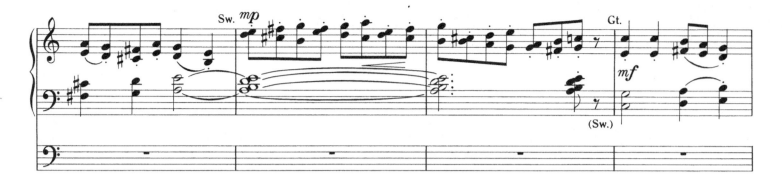

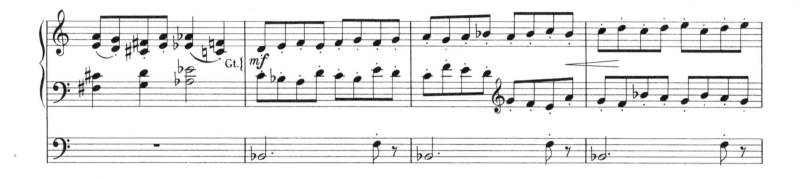

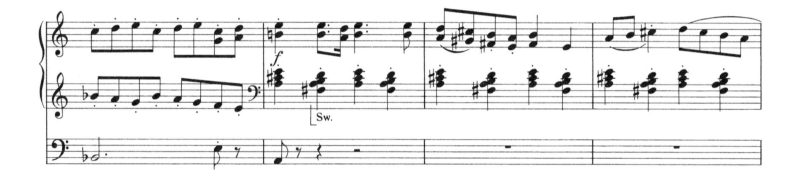

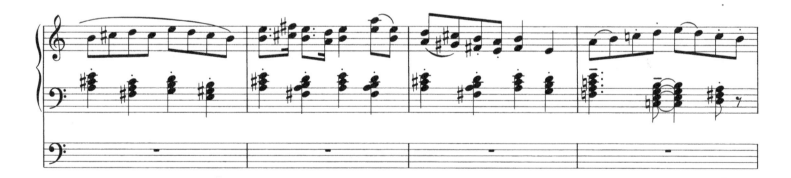

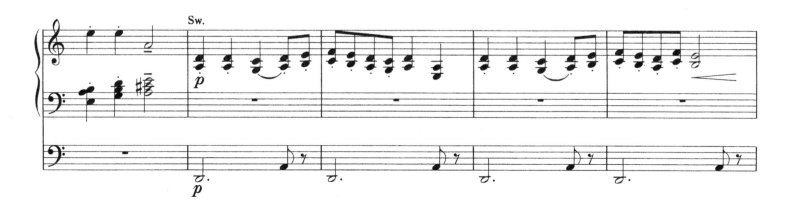

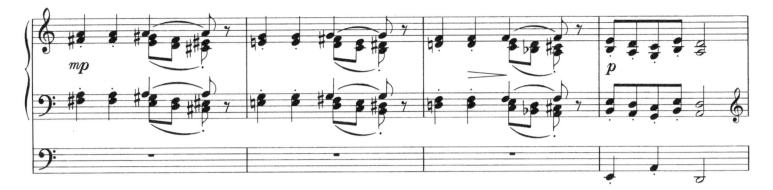

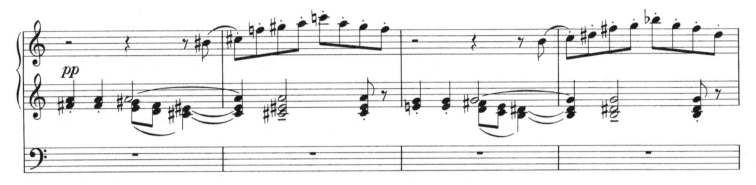

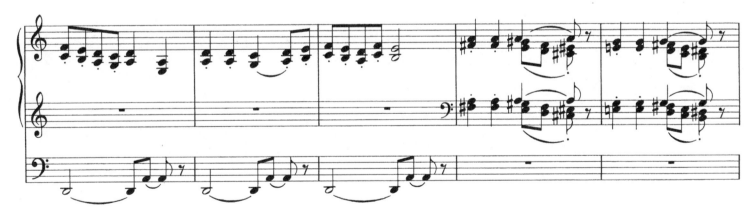

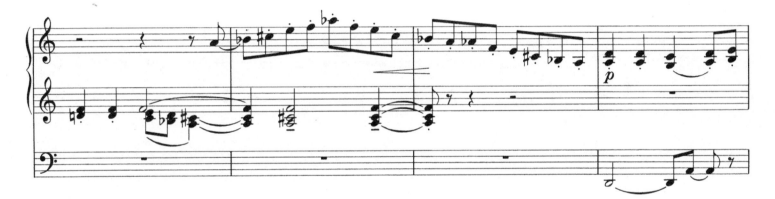

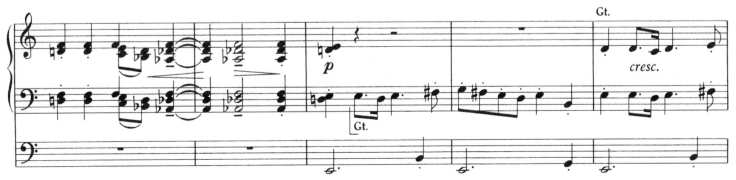

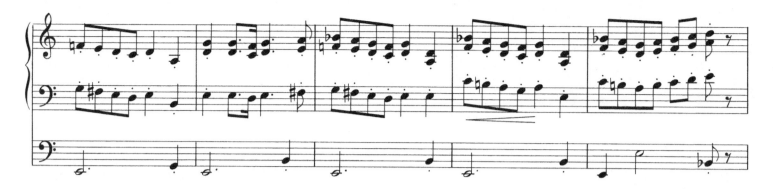

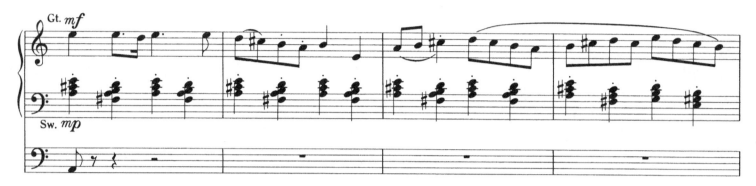

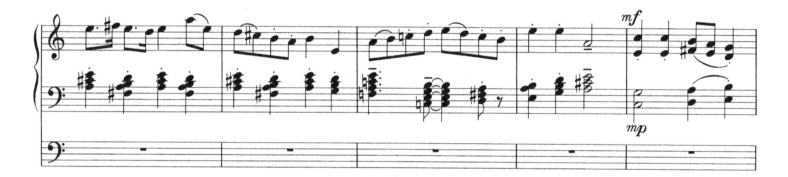

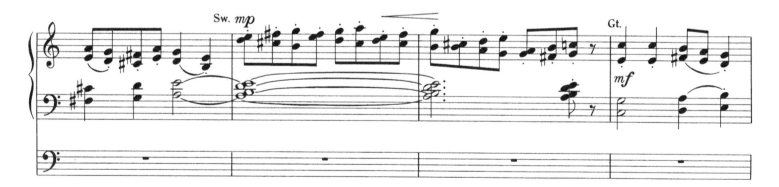

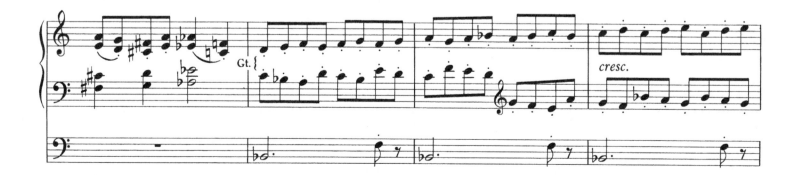

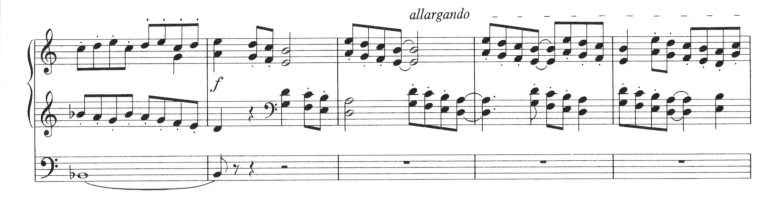

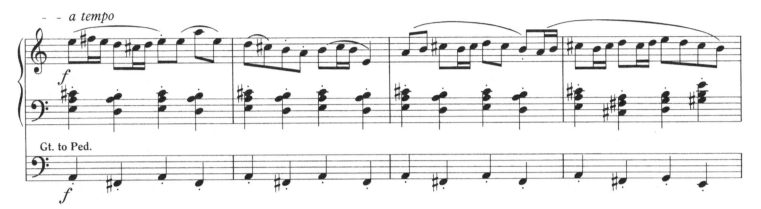

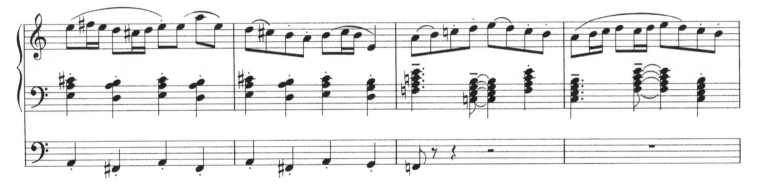

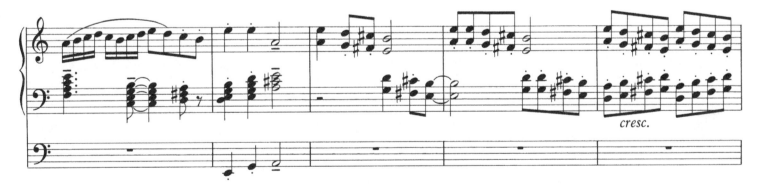

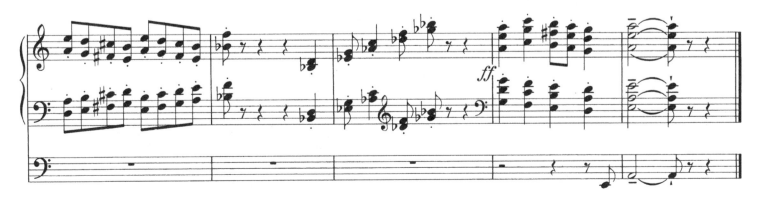